to Zoë, Kate, Alex, Pip, and Saff

Also available:
MY FIRST NURSERY STORIES

Hardback edition first published in Great Britain in 2007 by Andersen Press Ltd.,
20 Vauxhall Bridge Road, London SW1V 2SA.
Paperback edition first published in 2008.
Paperback and CD edition first published in 2009.
Published in Australia by Random House Australia Pty.,
Level 3, 100 Pacific Highway, North Sydney, NSW 2060.
Illustrations copyright © Tony Ross, 2007
The rights of Tony Ross to be identified as the illustrator of this work have
been asserted by him in accordance with the Copyright, Designs and Patents Act, 1988.
All rights reserved. Colour separated in Switzerland by Photolitho AG, Zürich.
Printed and bound in Singapore by Tien Wah Press.

10   9   8   7   6   5   4   3   2   1

British Library Cataloguing in Publication Data available.

ISBN 978 1 84270 705 0 (hardback edition)
ISBN 978 1 84270 746 3 (paperback edition)
ISBN 978 1 84270 973 3 (book and CD edition)

This book has been printed on acid-free paper

MY FAVOURITE NURSERY RHYMES

Selected and illustrated by

TONY ROSS

ANDERSEN PRESS

CONTENTS

"Grandad," said Nelly, "tell me a story, not a made-up one. One about real things."

"I don't know any stories about real things," said Grandad, scratching his nose, "but I do have this book of nursery rhymes. Some of those are about real things, real things that happened many years ago."

"What *are* nursery rhymes?" asked Nelly, looking very serious.

"Well," said Grandad, "when I was little, a billion years ago, I learned nursery rhymes at school, and from my Grandad, who was a trillion years old." As Nelly was only five, that seemed very old indeed. Grandad was thinking. "Mostly, they taught something," he said at last. "For instance, *Three Little Kittens* is about being rewarded if you behave properly."

"Like if I blow my nose, I get a bedtime story?" said Nelly.

"Exactly," said Grandad. "There is one about an owl who is wise because he listens, as well as making noise all the time."

"Oh!" said Nelly, being wise, and

not saying much. Grandad went on.

"Then some of them teach counting. *One, Two, Three, Four, Five* is one of those. *As I Was Going To St. Ives* is another, a harder one."

"I can count already!" said Nelly. "Almost up to a billion."

"And some of them are warnings of bad things that happened years and years ago," growled Grandad, holding his hands up like claws.

"OOOO!" squealed Nelly. "Tell me about those."

"*See-Saw Marjory Daw* is about children, not much older than you, who used to work in factories, and up chimneys. They earned a penny a day. *Ring-a-Ring o' Roses* was the ring of sores around the tummies of children who caught the plague. Then they sneezed and fell down for ever."

Nelly's eyes were wide like saucers. "What's the scariest one?" she whispered.

Grandad peered around the garden, just to make

sure no-one younger than four was listening.

"*Mary Mary* was the daughter of Henry the Eighth," he said softly, "and she was *very* contrary. That means difficult. The silver bells and cockle shells, and the row of little maids, were all quite awful."

"OOOO!" giggled Nelly. "I'm quite contrary sometimes. What's so awful about the bells and shells and little maids?"

Nothing in the garden stirred. Even the trees held their breath, waiting for an answer. Grandad stared at the book of nursery rhymes.

"I wonder if your mother knows," he said.

Three Little Kittens

Three little kittens they lost their mittens,
And they began to cry.
"Oh mother dear, we sadly fear,
That we have lost our mittens."
"What! Lost your mittens, you naughty kittens!
Then you shall have no pie."
"Miaow, miaow, miaow, now we shall have no pie."

The three little kittens, they found their mittens,
And they began to cry.
"Oh mother dear, see here, see here,
For we have found our mittens."
"Put on your mittens, you silly kittens,
And you shall have some pie."
"Miaow, miaow, miaow, now let us have some pie."

The three little kittens put on their mittens,
And soon ate up the pie.
"Oh mother dear, we greatly fear,
That we have soiled our mittens."
"What! Soiled your mittens, you naughty kittens!"
Then they began to cry.
"*Miaow, miaow, miaow.*" Then they began to sigh.

The three little kittens, they washed their mittens,
And hung them out to dry.
"Oh mother dear, do you not hear,
That we have washed our mittens."
"What! Washed your mittens, you are good kittens,
But I smell a rat close by."
"Miaow, miaow, miaow, we smell a rat nearby."

PUSSY CAT
PUSSY CAT

Pussy cat pussy cat where have you been?
I've been up to London to look at the Queen.

Pussy cat pussy cat what did you there?
I frightened a little mouse under her chair.

"MIAOW!"

What Are LITTLE BOYS Made Of?

What are little boys made of?
Snips and snails and puppy dogs' tails.
That's what little boys are made of!

What Are LITTLE GIRLS Made Of?

What are little girls made of?
Sugar and spice and all things nice.
That's what little girls are made of!

I HAD A LITTLE HEN

I had a little hen, the prettiest ever seen,

She washed up the dishes and kept the house clean.

She went to the mill to fetch us some flour,

And always got home in less than an hour.

She baked my bread, she brewed my ale,

She sat by the fire and told a fine tale.

THERE WAS A CROOKED MAN

There was a crooked man,
Who walked a crooked mile.
He found a crooked sixpence,
Upon a crooked stile.
He bought a crooked cat,
Which caught a crooked mouse,
And they all lived together
In a little crooked house.

Two Little Dicky Birds

Two little dicky birds sitting on a wall,
One named Peter, one named Paul.
Fly away Peter, fly away Paul,
Come back Peter, come back Paul.

Ring-a-Ring o' Roses

Ring-a-ring o' roses,
A pocket full of posies.
Atishoo, atishoo!
We all fall down.

This Little Piggy

This little piggy
went to market,

This little piggy
stayed at home.

This little piggy
had roast beef,

This little piggy
had none.

And this little piggy went,

"WEE wee wee,"
all the way home.

SING A SONG OF SIXPENCE

Sing a song of sixpence,
a pocket full of rye,
Four and twenty blackbirds,
baked in a pie.

When the pie was opened,
the birds began to sing,
Oh wasn't that a dainty dish
to set before the King?

The King was in his counting house,
counting out his money,
The Queen was in the parlour,
eating bread and honey.

The Maid was in the garden,
hanging out the clothes,
When down came a blackbird,
and pecked off her nose.

SEE-SAW MARJORY DAW

See-saw Marjory Daw,
Johnny shall have a new master.
He shall earn but a penny a day,
Because he can't work any faster.

JACK SPRAT

Jack Sprat could eat no fat,
His wife could eat no lean.
And so betwixt the two of them
They licked the platter clean.

ONE, TWO, THREE, FOUR, FIVE

One, two, three, four, five,

Once I caught a fish alive.

Six, seven, eight, nine, ten,

Then I let it go again.

Why did you let it go?

Because it bit my finger so.

Which finger did it bite?

This little finger on the right.

Ladybird, Ladybird!

Ladybird, Ladybird!
Fly away home.
Your house is on fire,
And your children are gone.
All except one,
And that's little Ann,
For she crept under
The frying pan.

POLLY
PUT THE
KETTLE ON

Polly put the kettle on,
Polly put the kettle on,
Polly put the kettle on,
We'll all have tea.

Sukey take it off again,
Sukey take it off again,
Sukey take it off again,
They've all gone away.

Little Jack Horner

Little Jack Horner sat in the corner,

Eating his Christmas pie.

He put in his thumb and pulled out a plum,

And said, "What a good boy am I!"

Mary, Mary

Mary, Mary, quite contrary,

How does your garden grow?

With silver bells and cockle shells,

And pretty maids all in a row.

OLD
MOTHER
HUBBARD

Old Mother Hubbard,

Went to the cupboard,

To get her poor doggie a bone.

When she got there,

The Cupboard was bare,

So the poor doggie had none.

Cry Baby Bunting

Cry Baby Bunting,
Daddy's gone a hunting,
Gone to fetch a rabbit skin,
To wrap the Baby Bunting in.
Cry Baby Bunting.

Little Tommy Tucker

Little Tommy Tucker, sings for his supper.
What shall we give him? Brown bread and butter.
How shall he cut it, without a knife?
How shall he marry, without a wife?

DOCTOR FOSTER

Doctor Foster went to Gloucester,
In a shower of rain.
He stepped in a puddle,
Right up to his middle,
And never went there again.

WISE
OLD OWL

A wise old owl
lived in an oak.
The more he saw,
the less he spoke.
The less he spoke,
the more he heard.
Why can't we all be like that wise old bird?

Mary
Had a Little Lamb

Mary had a little lamb,
its fleece was white as snow,
And everywhere that Mary went,
the lamb was sure to go.

It followed her to school one day,
which was against the rule.
It made the children laugh and play,
to see a lamb at school.

And so the teacher turned it out,
but still it lingered near,
And waited patiently about
'til Mary did appear.

"Why does the lamb love Mary so?"
the eager children cry.
"Why Mary loves the lamb, you know,"
the teacher did reply.

Little Miss Muffet

Little Miss Muffet sat on a tuffet,
Eating her curds and whey.
Along came a spider,
who sat down beside her,
And frightened Miss Muffet away.

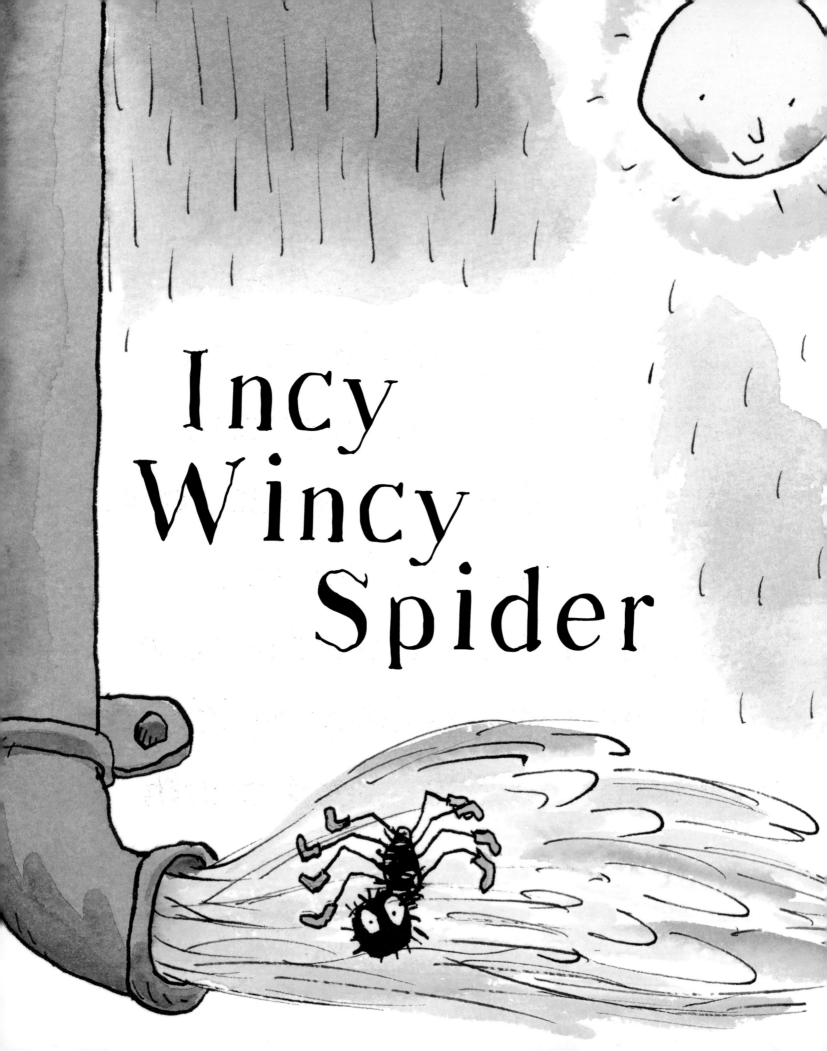

Incy
Wincy
Spider

Incy Wincy Spider,
Climbing up the spout.
Down came the rain,
And washed the spider out.
Out came the sun,
And dried up all the rain.
Now Incy Wincy Spider,
Went up the spout again.

Simple Simon

Simple Simon met a pieman
going to the fair.
Said Simple Simon to the pieman,
"Let me taste your ware."

Said the pieman to Simple Simon,
"Show me first your penny."
Said Simple Simon to the pieman,
"Sir, I have not any!"

Simple Simon went a fishing
for to catch a whale;
All the water he had got
was in his mother's pail.

Simple Simon went to look
if plums grew on a thistle;
He pricked his fingers very much,
Which made poor Simon whistle.

He went for water in a sieve
but soon it all fell through;
And now poor Simple Simon
bids you all adieu.

Jack and Jill

Jack and Jill went up the hill,

To fetch a pail of water.

Jack fell down and broke his crown,

And Jill came tumbling after.

Up Jack got, and home did trot,

As fast as he could caper.

He went to bed to mend his head,

With vinegar and brown paper.

Georgie Porgie

Georgie Porgie, pudding and pie,
Kissed the girls and made them cry.
When the boys came out to play,
Georgie Porgie ran away.

RIDE A COCK-HORSE

Ride a cock-horse to Banbury cross,
To see a fine lady upon a white horse.
With rings on her fingers and bells on her toes,
She shall have music wherever she goes.

HUMPTY DUMPTY

Humpty Dumpty sat on a wall,
Humpty Dumpty had a great fall.
All the King's horses and all the King's men
Couldn't put Humpty together again.

As I Was Going To St. Ives

As I was going to St. Ives,
I met a man with seven wives.
Each wife had seven sacks,
And in each sack were seven cats.
Each cat had seven kits.
Kits, cats, sacks, wives,
How many were going to St. Ives?

Baa Baa Black Sheep

Baa baa black sheep, have you any wool?
Yes sir, yes sir, three bags full.
One for the master, one for the dame,
And one for the little boy who lives down the lane.

DING
DONG
BELL

Ding dong bell,
Pussy's in the well.
Who put her in?
Little Johnny Flynn.
Who pulled her out?
Little Tommy Stout.
What a naughty boy was that,
Try to drown poor pussy cat,
Who never did him any harm,
But killed all the mice in the Farmer's barn!

RAIN, RAIN, GO AWAY

Rain, rain, go away,
Come again another day.
Little Johnny wants to play.
Rain, rain, go to Spain,
never show your face again.

For the Want of a Nail

For want of a nail
The shoe was lost,
For want of a shoe
The horse was lost,
For want of a horse
The rider was lost,
For want of a rider
The battle was lost,
For want of a battle
The kingdom was lost,
And all for the want of a nail.

GOOSEY GOOSEY GANDER

Goosey Goosey Gander,
Where shall I wander?
Upstairs, downstairs,
In my lady's chamber.
There I met an old man,
Who wouldn't say his prayers.
I took him by the left leg,
And threw him down the stairs.

THE MAN IN THE WILDERNESS

The man in the wilderness asked me,
How many strawberries grow in the sea?
I answered him as I thought good,
As many as herrings grow in the wood.

TOM, THE PIPER'S SON

Tom he was a piper's son,
He learned to play when he was young.
But all the tunes that he could play
Was "Over the hills and far away."

PAT-A-CAKE, PAT-A-CAKE

Pat-a-cake, Pat-a-cake, baker's man,
Bake me a cake as fast as you can.

Pat it and prick it, and mark it with a 'B',
And put it in the oven for baby and me.

ONE, TWO, BUCKLE MY SHOE

1, 2,
buckle my shoe,

3, 4,
shut the door,

5,6,
pick up sticks,

7,8,
lay them straight,

9,10,
a good fat hen.

Little Boy Blue

Little Boy Blue
come blow your horn,
The sheep's in the meadow,
the cow's in the corn.

But where is the boy
who looks after the sheep?
He's under a haystack fast asleep.
Will you wake him?
No, not I,
For if I do, he's sure to cry.

Little Robin Redbreast

Little Robin Redbreast sat upon a tree,
Up went pussy, and down went he:
Down came pussy, and away Robin ran:
Says Little Robin Redbreast, "Catch me if you can."
Little Robin Redbreast jumped upon a wall,
Pussy jumped after him and almost got a fall;
Little Robin chirped and sang, and what did pussy say?
Pussy said "Miaow!" and Robin jumped away.

THERE WAS AN OLD WOMAN
WHO LIVED IN A SHOE

There was an old woman who lived in a shoe,
She had so many children she didn't know what to do.
She gave them some broth, without any bread,
And she whipped them all soundly and sent them to bed!

Rock-a-Bye Baby

Rock-a-bye baby on the tree top,
When the wind blows, the cradle will rock.
When the bough breaks, the cradle will fall,
And down will come baby, cradle and all.

PETER PIPER

Peter Piper picked a peck of pickled pepper.

A peck of pickled pepper Peter Piper picked.

If Peter Piper picked a peck of pickled pepper,

Where's the peck of pickled pepper

Peter Piper picked?

PETER PETER PUMPKIN EATER

Peter Peter pumpkin eater,
Had a wife and couldn't keep her.
He put her in a pumpkin shell,
And there he kept her very well.

Hey Diddle Diddle

Hey diddle diddle,
the cat and the fiddle,
The cow jumped
over the moon.
The little dog laughed
to see such fun,
And the dish ran away
with the spoon.

THREE BLIND MICE

Three blind mice, three blind mice,
See how they run, see how they run.
They all ran after the farmer's wife,
Who cut off their tails with a carving knife.
Did you ever see such a thing in your life,
As three blind mice.

"Dad," called mum from the kitchen window.
"Have you seen the time? It's gone eight o'clock.
Nelly's got school in the morning."
"Hmmmm," said Grandad, and turned to the last
page of the book.
"Here's one last one:

Wee Willie Winkie runs through the town,
Upstairs and downstairs in his nightgown.
Tapping at the window
and crying through the lock,
Are all the children in their beds,
it's past eight o'clock!"

"It's past eight o'clock now, Grandad," whispered
Nelly, taking his hand.
"Do you think Wee Willie Winkie will tap at my
window tonight?"
There was a strange stillness in the garden, quiet
but for the bees and the breeze. It was one of
those evenings when anything could happen.
"I very much doubt it," said Grandad. "He must

be terribly old by now. Come on, Nell, time for bed."

In the warm evening quiet, the two of them went towards the house.

"I bet Grandad was Wee Willie Winkie," thought Nelly. "He is terribly old, *and* his name is William!"

INDEX OF FIRST LINES